ISBN-13: 978-1723234354
ISBN-10: 1723234354

Photo on the front cover: My mother and me.
Photo on the back cover: Me, neighbor Denny, and second cousins Gwennie and Jolie

Growing Up in The Burg

Mike Cohick

For my family

Table of Contents

Preface

This is a story about a small town where I grew up, as I remember how it existed during the years between 1945 and 1955. During that time I aged from seven to seventeen. It was a wonderful town for a kid. I will describe the town as it existed then, of course. However, the people living there at that time are the real story. I will concentrate on several of those people and how I remember certain events that happened back then.

What follows is a series of maybe not totally accurate descriptions of The Burg, some of its people, and some events that I remember. These recollections have been sifted through the aging gray cells of my brain for some 60 years, so please forgive any errors. I mean no offense. Nearly everything in this book is based on something that happened in or near The Burg when I was young. I don't refer to anybody's last names as I don't want to embarrass anyone. Those people whose stories are told, will know who they are. Other people don't really need to know.

When I have returned to The Burg as an adult, the conversation inevitably turned to the stories that happened years before. Those recollections have buttressed by own memories of things gone by. I thank all who participated in those many giggle sessions.

The Burg as it existed back then is, of course, no more. The reason I wrote this book is to preserve a few stories about The Burg and to document some anecdotes of how it was when I grew up there. It may not matter to most people. However, it matters to me.

I will start with some geography, first of the valley and then The Burg itself. The goal is to set the stage and allow the reader some framework in which to set the stories of my growing up. The ensuing chapters describe some events that happened in and around The Burg. The perspective is mine, of course. This is how I remember how these events happened.

Mike Cohick

July 4, 2018

Me and my lovely wife, Judy. She's a lucky lady because she's heard all these stories before.

Cy and his daughter, Connie at the Deer Park

Chapter 1

The Valley

The Creek that created the valley is not very long, maybe 25 miles in length. It struggles southward through the steep, wooded terrain in the northern part of the state. On its way, it carved out a narrow valley that has very little flat ground. What flat ground exists, is called bottom land. The sides of the valley are steep, and dense with trees. Animals like deer, bears, and rattlesnakes abound in these woods.

As The Creek flows south, it occasionally manages to make a piece of bottom land. In the early- and mid-1800's, settlers found these flat parcels and began establishing villages on them. Many of the other villages along The Creek never grew very big and remain small to this day. But The Burg became one of the largest with a population of nearly 400 people living there when I was a kid.

By its meandering, The Creek had managed to open maybe half a mile wide area of nearly flat land to its west - this became The Burg. The Creek moves from the east side of the valley, passed The Burg to the west, and moves back west once is it south of The Burg. To this day, you still have to cross a bridge over The Creek to leave The Burg.

Just before The Creek reaches the north end of The Burg, Second Fork joins it. Second Fork is The Creek's first significant tributary which enriches it with water gathered from another steep sided, densely wooded valley. This causes problems in the spring because as the snows melt, both branches of The Creek swell with melt water. When this melt water reaches The Burg, it sometimes spills over its banks and uses Main Street as a new path southward. There were two major floods of this type - one in 1936 and another in 1948. There probably have been more since then, but I haven't been around to witness them. Just south of The Burg, a second significant tributary joins The Creek called the First Fork.

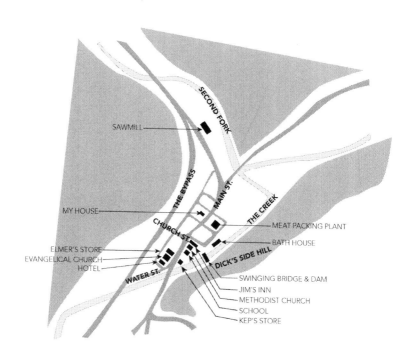

Map of The Burg, surrounding valley and sites mentioned in the book.

The Creek finally finds its destination about five miles south of The Burg where it flows into the River. This river is part of the principal drainage system of most of the northern and central parts of the state. The Creek is one of the smaller feeder streams that flows into the river after it collects the snow melt from the mountainous terrain that dominates this part of the state.

The Creek arrives late to the river. By the time the river meets the mouth of The Creek, many other creeks have already added their collection of melt water. In the spring, this river runs high and fast and sometimes actually flows northward back up The Creek. This sometimes isolates The Burg by flooding the highway. Because The Creek has carved such a narrow valley, it sometimes gets flooded from both directions - snow melt water coming down The Creek and river water coming back up The Creek.

In the winter, both the shallow Creek and the River would freeze over. However, the water in the river continued to flow under the ice and eventually that flow ebbed away. This left the river covered with ice from shore to shore with nothing under the ice. Ultimately, that ice would break - usually in the middle of the night and usually with an enormously loud crack that could be heard for miles. People in The Burg five miles north of the river often could hear it.

In the other seasons of the year, however, The Creek was a pleasant stream. It is not too deep, not too swift, and its bottom is covered with smoothed rocks that make good stepping stones. It is a very good stream for fishing and is filled with brook trout.

Those smooth rocks on the bottom of The Creek became building material during the Great Depression. (That was before my time). Thousands of these smooth rocks were used to build the town school and all the structures along The Creek including where my dad's cousin, Jim built a swimming emporium.

Along The Creek, mainly upstream from The Burg along both the main stream and Second Fork, are many camps and lodges that are devoted to hunting and fishing. These areas provide The Burg with a large economic boost as people from the big cities in the state flocked there to enjoy the appropriate season. Someone said that the area around The Burg has four seasons: getting ready for fishing season, fishing season, getting ready for hunting season, and hunting season. A lot of hunting and fishing occurred at these camps and lodges. However, as I recall, the main activity often was drinking beer out of sight of the wife.

The Creek carved both the valley and the nature of the people who live in the valley. It certainly has a strong influence on the people - including me - who lived in The Burg when I was a kid growing up.

Chapter 2

The Burg

The Burg is long north to south and skinny east to west. It might be half a mile wide between The Creek that flows to its east and the abruptly rising hills to its west. From north to south, it is about a mile and a half long. Well, a mile and a half if you measure from where Main Street splits from the Bypass at the north end of town to where it rejoins the Bypass at the south end of town.

For such a small town, The Burg had several small businesses. There were four small stores, all named after their owners. Tupper's was near the north end and served as the post office. Jim's Inn was in the center of town on the corner of Main and Church Streets. And at the south end of town across Main Street from each other, were Elmer's and Kep's which became the post office after Tupper's closed in the late 1940s. Tupper's also had a garage and a Packard dealership, but both went out of business during World War II.

At the far north end of Main Street was a saw mill. A bit farther south there was a grist mill. The grist mill owner built a millrace to divert Creek water to power his water wheel. The grist mill also went out of business early in my childhood, but south of the mill, out behind Gink's house, the millrace made the water pool. That pool of water became our hockey rink in the winter time.

Also on Main Street, was a meat packing plant and meat market retail outlet. My father and his two brothers – known everywhere and to everyone by their nicknames Mike, Jake, and Cy – were third generation owners of this business. The meat market was actually only half the building. The other half was living quarters for my Uncle Jake and his family. Later, it became living quarters for one of the packing plant's supervisors. In between the retail space and Uncle Jake's house was the office. In this office, I first learned to enjoy listening to baseball on the radio.

Down the street was Jim's Inn. Jim sold everything: meals, groceries, gasoline, fishing and hunting gear, farm supplies, bubble gum, mounted moose heads and sharp cheddar cheese which the locals called "rat cheese." It was always an adventure to walk through Jim's Inn. But Jim's Inn was really famous throughout the region for its ice cream.

On weekends, people would come from far and wide to sample Jim's Famous Homemade Ice Cream at a nickel a scoop. Celebrities even visited Jim's Inn and enjoyed the ice cream including James Cagney, Katherine Hepburn, Red Grange, and some of the most successful bootleggers of the Prohibition Era.

Across the street from Jim's was Vern's barber shop. I suppose it is typical of any small town for the barber shop to be the local meeting place and general hangout. Vern's barber shop certainly was that in The Burg. What Vern didn't have was coffee, so the townsfolk went to Jim's Inn for their

Kids waiting for the school bus outside Jim's Inn.

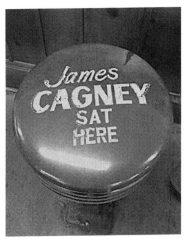 

The stools at the counter in Jim's Inn, where James Cagney and Kathryn Hepburn sat.

coffee. Above Vern's was the Odd Fellows Hall. However before I was old enough to become aware of such things, Odd Fellows Hall closed. The remainder of this building was used by Jim to sell appliances.

The X Brand Factory, which made pesticides, was located a couple of blocks further south. You probably noticed that there were no zoning laws in The Burg. This factory will be featured in a vignette later in the book.

At the lower end of town were Elmer's and Kep's stores. Elmer and Kep were related but did business separately. Elmer's store went under in the late 1940s. Elmer had a propensity to let his customers buy on credit but never collected. Elmer's customer appreciated this and shopped nowhere else. Kep's store lasted much longer. It became the teen hangout in my youth, primarily because my friend Dave, worked there in the evenings.

Next to Elmer's store was a tea room operated by Elmer's wife and daughter. I was never allowed in there, so I can't tell you much about it.

There were two churches, neither which was on Church Street - a Methodist church next to Jim's Inn and an Evangelical church next to Elmer's store. After I moved away, these churches merged into the Methodist church building, and the Evangelical church building next to Elmer's was converted into a residence. It still looks like a country church to this day.

The Methodist church was part of a three-church riding, located between The Burg and the mouth of The Creek. On Sunday, the one minister started at the mouth of The Creek and preached in that church beginning

The Methodist Church.

Here are the Hotel, the Evangelical Church and Elmer's Store where Main Street and Water Street meet and crosses The Creek.

9

at 8:30 a.m. He then moved upstream to the second church for a 9:30 a.m. service, and ended his morning in The Burg for service at 11:.00 a.m.

The parsonage was in The Burg just south of the meat market. The ministers changed frequently, so it seemed that a new family with new kids moved into the parsonage every few years.

At The Burg's Methodist church, there was a sanctuary and a meeting room on the main floor and a large open basement below. It was in the basement where monthly penny suppers were held to raise funds. Families would each bring casseroles and desserts, and parishioners would fill their plates at a penny per spoonful.

Just south of the Methodist church was the school. It was built by the Works Projects Administration or WPA in the 1930s, using the smooth stones found in The Creek. It started as a two-room school, but by the

The school faced with rocks from The Creek.

time I went there, only one room was used. My Aunt Mae was the teacher and she taught grades one through eight all in one room.

At the lower end of town, where Main Street crossed The Creek, there stood a hotel. It had about a dozen rooms, I don't know exactly how many because we kids were not allowed in the hotel. It had a large dining room and a huge front porch. The hotel was busy during hunting and fishing seasons, but generally was empty the rest of the year. To survive economically, the hotel dining room featured Sunday meals, specializing in chicken and waffles. Their culinary fame spread across the region, and throngs of patrons would show up every Sunday. When people couldn't be seated right away, they would wait on the front porch rocking in the rocking chairs. My mother would wait tables at the hotel each Sunday and said the tips were good. Many Sundays I would go to the hotel kitchen and have chicken and waffles for dinner.

At the top of Church Street where it joined the Bypass was Rocky's Garage and Gas Station. When it was built, it became another hangout for the teenage kids. In its parking lot there were always several cars in various stages of repair, or disrepair, as the case may be.

The rest of the town was filled up with houses, mainly two-story clapboard Gothic style. Nearly every one of them had a big front porch facing Main Street or Water Street - which split off from Main Street in front of the hotel and followed the course of The Creek. In the summer, these front porches were the place to be. Very few of these houses had any lawn space in front. The sidewalks paralleled the street with little to no space between the sidewalk and the porches. This feature made it difficult to move around town without everyone knowing where you were going or what you were doing.

Behind most houses were long back yards that, in earlier days, usually contained a chicken coop, an outhouse, a garden, a grassy area and a clothesline. Some houses also had a barn, which in my day had started to morph into a garage. At the end of the back lots were the alleys. The alleys paralleled Main Street on either side.

The Burg was and still is a small town. For the kids, the primary means of transportation was by bicycle and the entire town became our playground.

A few miles north of The Burg was a small hamlet with a collection of small frame houses, summer cabins, another saw mill, and The Burg's official baseball field.

South of town where First Fork joined The Creek, was another small hamlet which consisted of a few houses. Just to its south was Camp Kiwanis, a summer camp that brought kids from the cities out into the countryside.

Today, the saw mill, Jim's Inn (under new ownership), the meat packing plant (but not the retail outlet), and the Methodist church are all still active. The houses that were around when I was young are also still there, but you can count the newer houses on your fingers. Now, the town serves primarily as a quaint remote living area for commuters who work in the county seat 16 miles away.

When I was growing up in The Burg, there were a few families that dominated the town. My father was the second youngest of nine children

12

in one of those families and most of his siblings grew up and stayed in town. Collectively, they had 26 children, so many of the young people in town were cousins of mine.

It seemed like my cousins fell into two groups (or waves of birth). The first group were about ten years older than the second group - in which I would fall. I think the birth dearth gap in many of the families at that time coincided with the Great Depression.

Everyone knew everyone and most people were related. Nothing happened in the town that didn't get noticed and didn't get broadcast from one end of town to the other. Any kid that acted up or otherwise caused damage couldn't possibly get away with it. Somebody always saw and somebody always told. Because of this, kids were fairly well behaved.

Today many of the old families have died out, or their children have emigrated away from The Burg and the valley, like I did. Newer folks have moved in to take their place. It is still a small, pleasant town, but it is not the same.

Legend has it that my great-great grandfather found his way to The Burg while on the lam. He was running from the sheriff in a neighboring county who accused him of stealing a horse. Apparently, the valley and The Burg were sufficiently remote enough to be a good hiding place. He settled there and began a family and a business.

And so this story begins.

Chapter 3

Sing-Song
and Work-up

The school building was made of river stone, had a flagpole out front and a fairly large playground out back. The school initially had enough kids to fill its two rooms. However, that ended just as I reached first grade.

So, it became a one-room schoolhouse - in a two-room building. Grades one through eight were taught in one room by one teacher. The yearly number of students was consistently fewer than 35.

The teacher was my Aunt Mae. Her main teaching technique was rote learning. Rote learning is a memorization technique based on repetition. She also used the older kids to tutor (mentor? babysit?) the younger ones. Sometimes a trusted older student was asked to take younger students into the unused classroom and run them through their lessons.

Everything happened at the recitation benches at the front of the classroom. Aunt Mae (I was not allowed to call her that during the school day) would call the grade and class to the recitation benches.

"Fifth grade English. Rise, march, and be seated," she would say.

The Methodist Church and a rear view of the school with its playground. The hills to the west and north of The Burg stand out.

The students would then comply and the lesson would begin. Those not in that called class, stayed in their seats and did homework. Quiet was expected and was enforced by a hickory stick.

The hickory stick was about 18 inches long, two inches wide and ¾ inch thick. This stick was well used. Although it was not entirely accurate, we used to tell people, "The good kids get only one whack a day while the bad kids, like my cousin Bobby, get several."

Imagine being a student in that classroom for eight years. That means you got to hear each grade's school work eight times. It was all rote learning and group reciting of the rote learning, nearly always in sing-song fashion.

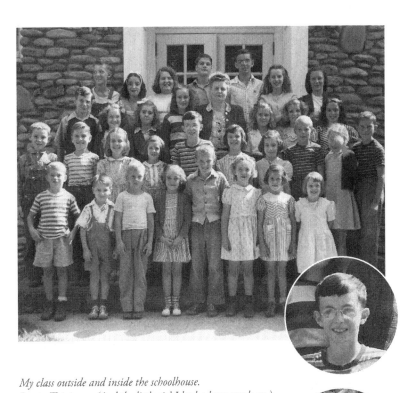

My class outside and inside the schoolhouse.
Insets: This is me. (And the little girl I had a huge crush on.)

What did we learn? Well, we started in first grade with a spelling list.

a

an: a-n

it: i-t

has: h-a-s

see: s-e-e

fan: f-a-n

the: t-h-e

bird: b-i-r-d

in: i-n

tree: t-r-e-e

man: m-a-n

And that's about as much of the first grade litany as I remember after 70 years.

The list expanded each year with more words learned sing-song. We learned penmanship and cursive using ink pens dipped in ink wells. We studied geography including all 48 states and capitals and all the nations of the world and their capitals each sung in a precise order. We learned about history including the names of Spanish, French, English, and Dutch explorers their discoveries and the dates on which they discovered it. We learned the presidents from Washington to Truman. We studied historical battles and wars including their dates and locations. We studied math including the multiplication tables in sing-song: 1 times 2 is 2; 2 times 2 is 4; etc. all the way through 12 times 12 is 144. And we studied reading which included memorizing one new poem each month. All of this was learned by rote and recited in song back to the teacher in unison by the whole class.

Everyone walked to school, in all kinds of weather, including the teacher who lived at the far upper end of The Burg. School started with the Pledge of Allegiance at 9:00 a.m. Classes went until 10:30 a.m. followed by a 15-minute recess. Then there was more class work until noon when everyone went home for lunch. School resumed at 1:00 p.m. until afternoon recess at 2:30 p.m. After recess, school went until 4:00 p.m.

Recess was special. We really had no playground equipment, so we made do with some volunteered things. Baseball was big in The Burg, so the centerpiece of recess was often a baseball game. Nearly all the kids played.

We played a variation of the game we called "work-up." Three kids were batters and the rest of the kids were fielders. A batter would bat until he or she was out. Then he or she became the last fielder, and all the fielders moved up one position. The catcher would then became the replacement batter, the pitcher became the catcher, the first baseman became the pitcher and so on.

The only exception was if a fielder caught a fly ball, then the fielder and the batter would change places. When recess ended, everyone remembered what position he or she was occupying, and the game resumed at the next recess. This method began when the school year started the day after Labor Day and continued until snow fell and stayed. Then the game was suspended until spring when it started up again.

Recess continued through the winter in the snow. The game was changed to "fox and geese." It operated much the same way as "work-up." First, a huge circle was tramped out in the snow. Then, two paths were tramped at right angles to each other, each of which intersected the circle and made a cross inside the circle.

The game was played much like tag. There was a fox and his or her job was to catch the geese. The intersections of the stomped out paths with themselves and with the circle were considered "safe spots" where geese couldn't be caught by the fox. No more than two geese could be at an intersection at one time.

When the fox caught a goose, they exchanged positions, and there was a new fox. When recess ended, everyone remembered where they were and at the next recess, assumed that position and the game resumed. This went on from when the snow fell and stayed until the snow melted, at which time, baseball "work-up" began again.

Did the kids learn anything? Is rote a good way to learn? Or was any learning due to the many years of repetitive hearing of the lessons? In my experience, the times tables, the explorers, the states and capitals, the nations and their capitals, and several of the poems (or at least pieces of them) are instantly available to me all these years later. Some of my cousins say the same thing.

However, my penmanship never really got any good. My cursive handwriting is still terrible. Maybe it's because I'm left handed.

These are some of my school photos.

Six years old.

12 years old.

14 years old.

My high school senior yearbook picture.

Chapter 4

George and X-Brand

George lived in the house next to the school. He also owned a vacant lot across Main Street. George was the typical entrepreneurial type and started several businesses throughout the years. When I was ten, George began building a concrete block structure on the vacant lot with the intent to manufacture poisonous chemicals. He planned on marketing those chemicals under the unusual name, "X Brand."

There were no zoning restrictions in The Burg. Despite the fact that George was planning on manufacturing poisonous chemicals, there were no requirements to acquire permits or seek approval from any authority organizations.

George didn't tell anyone in town what he was doing, but the construction became the hot topic over coffee at Jim's Inn. The curious inhabitants of The Burg wanted to know, "What was George building? What was he going to do in the building?"

Construction started in the spring just after the snow finally melted. Progress was slow. Tiers of concrete blocks went up. Window frames were installed. The coffee drinkers at Jim's Inn monitored the slow progress and

My father in the chicken coop behind our house. Years later, my maternal uncle Bill would develop a fabulous garden here due to the years of built up chicken droppings.

made wild conjectures on what was going on. George remained silent. Spring turned to summer. Summer turned to fall.

As fall progressed, one morning my father asserted at the morning coffee meeting, "If George gets the roof on that building before snow falls, I'll change my name to Olmstead."

Everyone murmured in agreement and ordered another cup of coffee.

September came and went and then October. Progress on George's building continued its slow pace. Then one day in late October, the roof was put on the building. Snow had not begun to fall.

My second cousin, Buddy, who was eight years older than me, piped up at the coffee drinkers meeting that the roof was in place and snow had not come. Then he reminded everyone of my father's pledge.

From that day onward, Buddy called my father Olmstead. And by extension, I got tagged with the name, too.

George's X Brand poisons were a commercial failure. Manufacturing ceased after a year. The factory sat empty for a long time. No one was concerned about toxic spills or environmental contamination.

Several years after George passed away, his daughter gutted the factory and transformed it into two apartments.

A minor side point. George's house was next to the school and a tall hedge separated his backyard from the school's playground. During the ongoing "work-up" baseball game, sometimes batters would hit the ball over the hedge in right field into George's back yard. George did not like that. Since there was only one ball, this required someone to crawl through the hedge to recover the ball. Therefore, we created a new rule for "work-up." Over the hedge was out. And we created a similar rule for left field where the outer boundary of the school yard was the millrace. A hit into the millrace was also out.

Hitting the ball into the millrace was a bigger problem than over the hedge. A ball landing in the millrace moved downstream swiftly. All the kids would hurry along the millrace to retrieve the only ball before the millrace joined The Creek. If we lost the ball, then the "work-up" baseball game was over until somebody brought a new ball to school.

Oh, one more fact about George. In 1948, George ran for President of the United States.

He lost.

Chapter 5

My Grandfather

My paternal grandparents lived on Main Street in the middle of The Burg, just two houses north of Jim's Inn. My grandfather had owned the meat packing plant in town which before he retired, he turned the business over to his three sons - Jake, Cy and Mike.

In his retirement, my grandfather liked to spend most of his day on his large front porch presiding over the daily movements up and down Main Street. The Burg was essentially a one street town, so if anyone was going to move around town, he or she would have to use Main Street and go past his house. That included all of his grandchildren, including me.

All the grandchildren called my grandfather, "Pop-poo." Pop-poo was very prim and straight laced. He would have made a terrific Victorian. Just to give you an indication, at precisely at 6 p.m. every evening, he would sit at the dining table, knife in one hand and fork in the other, and expect his wife (whom the grandchildren called "Mom-poo") to have dinner on the table.

There is a old story, that one day Mom-poo got home late from the city. She raced into the kitchen while still wearing her go-to-town hat and

My grandfather's house. Standing from left to right: Pop-poo, Lester, Mae, Martha, Lotte (a live-in companion for Mom-poo), Mom-poo with Clarice in her arms, and Roy. Sitting from left to right: Mike, Jake and Cy. Not pictured: Ruth.

having her purse slung over her shoulder to get Pop-poo's dinner on the table in time.

Pop-poo did not like to see idleness in anyone (except maybe himself). When he spied one of his grandchildren coming up or down Main Street, he would summon the child to the porch and conjure up a chore for that child to do. And none of us were bold enough to refuse such a request.

One day, I was going to the lower end of The Burg to play with my best friend, Max. Pop-poo saw me coming and summoned me to the front porch. Of course, I went. He told me there was a lot of firewood piled up, out back, near the kitchen door and I should rack it up, so that his wife could move it more easily to fuel the wood stove in the kitchen.

So, I went to the back of the house and stacked fire wood – and there was a lot of wood. It took nearly an hour. When I finished and received Pop-poo's approval, he gave me a nickel and told me to go to Jim's Inn and buy a one-scoop ice cream cone.

That was not much of a reward for the hard work done, but it was typical. The grandchildren quickly caught on to this pattern, and we began to come up with ways of navigating around The Burg not to be detected by Pop-poo. We skulked down the back alleys and even climbed the hill up to the Bypass to avoid him.

All homes burned wood in their kitchen stoves until the electric stove became commonplace

Mom-poo and Pop-poo in their later years.

I don't mean for this story to paint Pop-poo as an ogre or an uncaring grandparent - it was just his way. Surely, he thought that he was improving our lives by filling those idle moments with productive things to do.

He somehow figured that I was a person who always wanted to learn. He gave me some of his books, including a WPA history of the county - which featured him of course. One of the books I especially treasured was a World Atlas. From it, I began to develop a life-long love of maps.

This turned out to be tremendous help in my professional life as I traveled and worked around the world extensively as an adult. I learned a lot from that atlas, despite some of it being woefully out of date. The publishing date for the atlas was before World War I. In the atlas, Austria-Hungary and the Ottoman Empire dominated the old world maps. And in the new world, there were only 45 states - Arizona, New Mexico, Oklahoma, Hawaii and Alaska were still territories.

Every autumn, Mom-poo and Pop-poo would gather in the backyard with several of the neighbors. They would build a large fire pit and put a huge iron cauldron on top. In the cauldron, Mom-poo would mix apple mash, sugar, water and spices.

Uncle Dick, Pop-poo's brother, ran the ciderpress for his nephew as one of the many side business of Jim's Inn. Apple mash was what was left after apples go through a ciderpress.

Once all these ingredients were in the cauldron, the fire was lit and everyone took turns stirring the mixture. It took hours until the heat turned the spiced apple mash to a caramelized brown with a smooth consistency.

The apple butter was then placed in mason jars and sealed, so it could be used throughout the coming year. Enough apple butter was made for nearly all the extended family and for the families of the neighbors who helped.

Canning fruits and vegetables for the coming year was a common event everywhere in The Burg.

Mom-poo, Pop-poo and a neighbor stirring the apple butter in the back yard.

Chapter 6

The Ivaroy

My father was one of nine children - eighth in line, nearly the youngest. Of the nine, seven stayed in The Burg after they married and raised their families. Growing up, there were 26 of us cousins.

The second oldest of Pop-poo's children was Roy. Roy was a school teacher and a minister. As a teacher, he taught my dad, his brother, but he had retired from being a minister before I was old enough to be aware.

Roy married Iva, and they had five children: Bill, Katherine, Harold (who they called Bish), James and Mary Ruth. Mary Ruth, the youngest, was two years older than me.

Roy lived across Main Street and up a couple of houses from us. His house backed onto the millrace below the hockey rink pool. His property was verdant and a pleasant place to be on a warm summer's day.

As I said, Roy was retired. I was about ten. Many afternoons, I walked over to Roy's house, and we played anagrams. Anagrams was an ancestor to Scrabble. The main differences were that there was no board, no multiple word scores and no points on the letters. Also, there were a lot more tiles.

33

Roy would put the tiles in a box, mix them up, and spill out two dozen on the table. The object was to use all the letters on the table. Whoever used up the last letters got points. Then another dozen letters were dumped out. Roy played a tough game. It was in these sessions that I learned words like viz, syzygy and chiffon.

One spring, Roy hired some workmen to build an outdoor pavilion in his back yard. It had a concrete floor, four sturdy pillars holding up a rainproof roof, a barbecue at one end, and a table with parallel benches at the other end. It looked out across the heavily flowered backyard toward the millrace and the grove of trees beyond. It was a beautiful place. Roy christened it the "Ivaroy," amalgamating his name and his wife's name.

That summer the Ivaroy was the sensation of The Burg. Everyone had to come by and admire it. Roy and I moved our anagrams game outside to the Ivaroy for the rest of the summer.

Roy's younger brother, Jake, came by to check out this marvelous structure. Jake was building a new house at the far north end of The Burg, where Main Street rejoined the Bypass. Jake was smitten by the Ivaroy. He directed the builders to replicate it at his new home. When Jake and his family moved in, they held an open house. Jake proudly showed off the new pavilion in his back yard.

"This is my Ivaroy," he said.

Someone pointed out that "Ivaroy" was not a proper name for such a structure. They told Jake that his brother had created the term using his and his wife's names.

Jake piped up, "It's still the Ivaroy," he said. "That sounds so much better than calling it after my wife and me, the Beulahjake."

Chapter 7

Hot Dogs

Just across the street from our house sat the meat packing plant and retail outlet. My father, Mike, and his two brothers, Jake and Cy, owned and operated the plant. Mike was in charge of the slaughterhouse. Jake was in charge of processed meat products. Cy was in charge of sales. As it was my father's business, the meat packing plant played a significant role in my youth.

My first memory of the business was visiting Bill after school. Bill ran the retail outlet. When there were no customers, Bill would sit in the office next door to the retail outlet and listen to the radio.

During these afternoon visits, Bill and I would listen to the radio. Mostly we listened to radio soap operas like *The Guiding Light*, *Stella Dallas*, *Lorenzo Jones*.[1] In the fall, we listened to the World Series. In 1947, the New York Yankees played the Brooklyn Dodgers in the World Series. The Yankees, who my dad detested, were a perennial powerhouse and the Dodgers, who my dad loved, were "Dem Bums" who never amounted to much. This time, Brooklyn took the Yankees to a full seven games before losing. And it was that year that I became a radio sports fan.

---

1. *The Guiding Light* broadcast 15-minute episodes which was adapted to television in 1952. *Stella Dallas* was a 15-minute soap opera based on the novel by the same name. *Lorenzo Jones* was a 15-minute comedy soap opera.

The meat market retail store after it was expanded. Originally, the market consisted of only the two leftmost windows. The rest of the building was a residence. Dick's Side Hill looms behind it.

This fleet of trucks delivered meat to restaurants throughout the northern part of the state. Left to right, my father, Bill (Roy's son) and Cy.

The packing plant had three parts: the slaughterhouse, the cold lockers which were called coolers, and the processing area which was brand new. When the new processing area was completed, it became Jake's pride and joy. This area was where Jake manufactured processed meats like bologna, cold cuts, sausage and hot dogs. There were huge mixing machines, pressure pumps, overhead railings that would take racks of processed goods to the hickory-fired smoke houses.

One of the guys who worked for Jake, was named Allen. Allen was a jack-of-all-trades but master of none. Allen lived with a woman named Blanche. Jake kept pestering Allen to "make an honest woman out of Blanche" and marry her.

When Allen finally gave in and asked Blanche to marry him, it happened to coincide with the grand opening of the new processing area. So Jake

My great-great grandfather started the business in 1884. His nickname was Shiner. For years, the company used the term Shiner Brand.

arranged to have the wedding ceremony in the new area. The local minister, the whole meat packing crew and indeed the whole town was invited.

The wedding took place on a beautiful, sunny day. Everyone came. The place was packed with people and we kids were running around everywhere. That night, The Burg treated the newlyweds Allen and Blanche to a chivaree[2], or as they called it, a belling.

During the first week of summer vacation when I was 14, I was sitting on my front porch when Del, the plant foreman walked across the street with a message. He said that my dad wanted me to get to the plant and start work.

I followed Del to the plant. I put on a heavy sweater, a winter coat and a white smock and entered the cooler where hot dogs were prepared for sale.

There were other teenagers already working, and they gave me some on-the-job training. The hot dogs came in long strings of 100 encased in cellophane. The strings of dogs were then draped on racks suspended from the overhead rails. They had been hickory smoked the day before and were now chilling in the 25 degree Fahrenheit cooler.

> Aside: How hot dogs are made. First, a meat slurry was made. After the meat slurry was thoroughly mixed, it was placed in a pressurized pump. A 50-foot long cellophane tube was placed over the nozzle of the pump. Someone would turn on the machine and the pressure from the pump would force the slurry into the cellophane tube. The tube full of slurry would pass through another machine which would tie string every six

2. A chivaree is a German folk custom in which a mock parade is staged and the crowd makes as much noise as possible banging on pots and pans.

inches, thus making each hot dog. The connected hot dogs was gathered by a worker, draped over a pole, and placed on the rack which when full, would take the uncooked hot dogs to the smoker.

My job, and the job of the other teens, was skinning wieners. Skinning wieners was to remove the cellophane casing from the smoked hot dogs and arrange the finished hot dogs in boxes for shipment to the customers. We cut the casing where the string was tied with a paring knife. Then in one motion, stripped off the cellophane and put the hot dog in the box.

With practice, we all got to be very good. My productivity maxed out at about 120 pounds of hot dogs per hour.

We tended to get into a rhythm. Grab the casing. Make the cut. Pull off the cellophane. Put the hot dog into the box. Repeat. Repeat again. And again. And again. Ad infinitum. Ad nauseam.

Our day began at 6 a.m. and ended at 6 p.m. with an hour for lunch. I was paid minimum wage, which at the time was 50 cents per hour. Eleven hours a day, five and a half days a week (on Saturdays we knocked off at noon) came to 60 hours each week. That yielded, pretax and pre FICA, $30 each week.

We were teenagers with few skills but with some muscle on our backs. Therefore, if some task needed to be done outside the cooler, the foreman would often commandeer one or more of us to do it. Since we knew that we would be outside for only a little bit of time, we did not take off our cold weather cooler gear.

We would load trucks, offload trucks, sweep up messes, run errands, and whatever else needed to be done, all while looking like Nanook of the North[3] in the 80 to 90 degree weather. We would build up a good sweat under our clothes and then return to the cooler. What a wonderful way to spend a summer vacation.

Many of my cousins - girls included - skinned wieners too. Some cousins lasted a long time, while others were smart enough to quit and go do other things.

After a couple of years, my pay was increased to the new minimum wage of 75 cents per hour ($45 each week). When this happened, I learned my first lesson in economics. When the minimum wage was increased, the plant laid off several of the workers making minimum wage. What work they had been doing was simply parceled out to the remaining employees. Those still employed got a raise; those laid off got nothing.

This business philosophy is still true today. When minimum wage is increased, low skill jobs disappear.

When fall came and I had to go to back to school, I would work at the plant from 6 a.m. to 8 a.m. The bus would pick up the high school kids in front of Jim's Inn at 8:15 a.m. After school I would return and work from 4 p.m. to 6 p.m. I also began to clerk at the retail outlet Friday nights until 9 p.m. and all day Saturday.

One nice thing about working at the plant was that we got breakfast. Jake would cook up whatever meats came back unsold on the wholesale trucks

3. *Nanook of the North: A Story of Love and Life in the Actual Arctic* is a 1922 silent documentary.

the night before. He cooked in a huge cauldron normally used to render lard. The entire crew ate breakfast this way.

I became well known on the school bus as the guy with a pork chop in each hand as I boarded the bus. I ate this wonderful hot breakfast on my way to school.

Chapter 8

Fred

My uncle Cy and his wife, known to everyone as Clix, wanted a place where they could "get away." They owned a cabin just to the north of The Burg along Second Fork of The Creek. It was set back off the highway in a grove of tall trees. The trees placed the cabin forever in the shade - a positive attribute in the summer. Taking after the prevailing method of naming things in The Burg, they called their cabin the Clixcy.

Later, Cy found another summer place for sale about twelve miles north of The Burg. This was a stone house, situated at the far edge of a large field at The Creek's edge. The state highway was nestled in between the far side of the field and a steep, wooded hillside. A dirt road connected the house to the state highway. Cy bought this property and called it "The Ranch."

The Ranch consisted of a two story, ranch house with two bedrooms and a bath upstairs and a kitchen and living room downstairs. Cy funded a full-length, two-story expansion of the original house. Downstairs he added a large sun room that ran the length of the house and looked out over The Creek. Upstairs he added a full-length bunk room. There was also small barn to store tools and an in-ground swimming pool. Cy installed flood lights across the front of the house pointing into the large field. These

The Ranch, located several miles north of The Burg.

lights enabled nighttime deer spotting, a favorite avocation of Cy and his visitors.

Cy's family used The Ranch for many things. His daughters, Carolyn, Connie, Claramae, and Cynthia - also known as The Four C's - used The Ranch for sorority parties and such goings on when they were in college. His extended family held outings there many times during the summer.

But the use of The Ranch I want to talk about was when Cy invited his buddies and business associates for an evening of good food, drink and deer spotting.

The Ranch was somewhat isolated which made Cy uncomfortable leaving it unoccupied for long periods of time. Enter Fred.

Fred was a widower who had retired but still did odd jobs around The Burg. Cy asked Fred to move in at The Ranch and become its caretaker.

Also, Fred could work as the cook when Cy brought his cronies up to The Ranch. Fred agreed, and this symbiotic relationship flourished.

It was late one afternoon when Cy decided to host several of his friends and associates at The Ranch. He called Fred and notified him that several people were coming and they needed to be fed. It was too late for Fred to make a trip to the grocery store, so he had to improvise using what was stocked on hand. Working as fast as he could, Fred came up with a presentable meal that would be ready when the guests arrived. One of the side dishes for this meal was to be baked corn - a simple dish that uses two cans of creamed corn.

As the feast was served, several of the guests began to comment on one of the dishes. They kept saying how good it was, and how they didn't think they ever had anything like it before. They complimented Cy and Fred for this surprisingly good dish.

Later as Fred was cleaning up, he noticed that the two empty cans had contained crushed pineapple, not creamed corn. In his haste, Fred did not inspect the cans he pulled off the shelf. Fred had inadvertently created baked pineapple.

Since it was such a hit, Fred went on to teach my mother how to make baked pineapple. My mother taught it to my wife. My wife taught it to my daughter.

It is a favorite side dish of our family. I think it could become a favorite side dish of yours, too. I give you the recipe.

Bon appétit!

Baked Pineapple

Ingredients
 1 can crushed pineapple (15-16 ounces)
 2 Tbsp flour
 1/2 cup sugar
 1 egg
 Pinch of salt
 Cinnamon (to taste)

Directions
 Preheat the oven to 350 degrees.

 Mix ingredients together.

 Put into a greased 8 inch casserole dish.

 Sprinkle cinnamon on top.

 Bake for 30-45 minutes until mixture is more solid
 than liquid. It shouldn't jiggle much.

Chapter 9

Decoration Day

In other parts of the country, the last Monday in May is Memorial Day. In The Burg when I was growing up, everyone called it Decoration Day. Decoration Day was, in my opinion, the biggest summertime holiday, far outpacing Independence Day. It signaled the end of the school year and the beginning of freedom for all the children in town. Also, it was most likely the first really nice weekend of the year after the nastiness of winter and the wetness of spring.

The Burg celebrated Decoration Day in a big way culminating in a town parade. All the kids decorated their bikes with streamers. People would shine up their old, classic vehicles. Horse owners rode their faithful steeds. The high school band would cue up the patriotic music.

Everybody who was not in the parade would watch from their front porches. My uncle Roy and Mary, who lived two doors down, took special interest in the horses. Both Roy and Mary would be at the ready, coal shovel and bucket in hand, ready to pounce if any horse decided to leave droppings along the parade route in front of their houses.

When such an event happened, they would each race off their porch and zero in on the treasure, determined to beat the other and claim the prize. If their race ended in a tie, they would stand in the middle of the street and argue over whom should be declared the winner. If they were successful, they would "win" high quality, fresh fertilizer for their respective gardens. Both Roy and Mary had dynamite gardens in their back yards, filled with vegetables and flowers.

At my house, my mother especially liked Decoration Day, because it often coincided with her birthday - May 30. For years, she asserted that the parade was in her honor, not because of the national holiday.

Years later on her 70th birthday, the high school band stopped in front of my mother's house, turned to face her, and played "Happy Birthday." Everyone who witnessed it, said she had the biggest grin.

This town cornet band marched in the Decoration Day parade before World War II. In my day, they were replaced with the area's high school marching band.

The Decoration Day Parade started at the church near Jim's Inn. It marched northward along Main Street to the top of The Burg. Once at the north end of town, it would reverse direction and proceed southward the length of the town, across the bridge in front of the hotel, and to the cemetery on the hill near the end of town.

It was at the cemetery where the actual decorating of Decoration Day occurred. Each gravesite would be decorated with flowers. Graves of soldiers from the Civil War and both World Wars would be given small flags. Most of the town's inhabitants followed the parade to the cemetery and helped to decorate the graves.

Then the speeches would begin. The centerpiece of the speeches was the Gettysburg Address recited by Rocky, the local justice of the peace. He built up a stentorian tone and bellowed out the speech, not humbly like Abraham Lincoln did the first time these words were spoken.

Rocky lived at and ran the hotel for several years. His favorite thing at the hotel were the rocking chairs on the front porch. He loved the rocking chairs. If anyone wanted to talk, they could always find Rocky sitting on the porch in a rocking chair. Even we kids liked to talk to Rocky.

Rocky was married to Nellie, a superstar in her own right. One thing I remember about Nellie was her ability to recite from memory the epic "Thanatopsis." Thanatopsis is an 81-line poem written by William Cullen Bryant in 1817. The title comes from the Greek word thanatos which means death, and opsis which means sight.

Like all others of her era, Nellie was required to memorize poetry like this when she was in elementary school. Imagine if you had been required to memorize poetry like this when you were in elementary school. Or better yet, try to imagine current elementary school children memorizing such a poem.

Thanatopsis
William Cullen Bryant

To him who in the love of Nature holds

Communion with her visible forms, she speaks

A various language; for his gayer hours

She has a voice of gladness, and a smile

And eloquence of beauty, and she glides

Into his darker musings, with a mild

And healing sympathy, that steals away

Their sharpness, ere he is aware. When thoughts

Of the last bitter hour come like a blight

Over thy spirit, and sad images

Of the stern agony, and shroud, and pall,

And breathless darkness, and the narrow house,

Make thee to shudder, and grow sick at heart;—

Go forth, under the open sky, and list

To Nature's teachings, while from all around—

Earth and her waters, and the depths of air—

Comes a still voice—

No rush, you can Google the rest at your leisure.

Chapter 10

Dick's Side Hill

Who was Dick? Why did he have a side hill? And why just one side, not both? The story begins about a decade before I was born. Let me provide some background before I describe the role Dick's Side Hill played in my childhood.

Dick was not his real name, but a nickname which people in The Burg were known to appended to just about everyone in that era. His real name was Lawrence.

My grandfather, Pop-poo, had two brothers, John and Dick. Dick never married, and after John died, Dick took over raising John's kids. One of John's kids was named Jim who would grow up to be the proprietor of Jim's Inn.

When Jim married and started a family, Dick moved in with them and lived with them for the rest of his life. As he was Jim's uncle, he was called Uncle Dick by everyone in town.

In the 1930s, Jim's Inn became quite successful. People came from all over the county for Jim's Famous Homemade Ice Cream. Jim began to branch

Jim's Inn, in the late 1930's early 1940's.

out into other enterprises. As Jim's business enterprises grew, Dick became the all-around handyman and ran many of Jim's businesses.

Jim was renovating and expanding his house to make it more modernized. He liked the look of the stonework on the school house. So, Jim commissioned a local stone mason, Charlie, to face his clapboard house with the same stone. And Charlie's stonework became a signature element of many of Jim's enterprises over the next decade.

During the expansion of the house, Dick built behind the house a summer kitchen and Charlie faced it with the stone. Jim's newly refurbished home sat alongside The Creek, and across The Creek was a steep, heavily forested hillside that Jim also owned. That became known as Dick's Side Hill.

In the 1930s, Jim was inspired by the massive Tennessee Valley Authority (TVA) flood control projects some of which generated electricity. He obtained state permission to build a dam on The Creek to generate electricity for his home and his businesses. Building the dam created a wide lake-like expanse just upstream. Next to the dam, Jim built a

The dam and the swinging bridge that gave access to Dick's Side Hill.

powerhouse which held the electricity generator. Water from above the dam flowed into the powerhouse and was expelled into a millrace that ran alongside the school before rejoining The Creek below the dam.

Once the dam was in place, Jim created two spectacular recreational areas. First along the lake-like expanse, he had Charlie build a stone-clad bathhouse complete with changing rooms and showers. Next to the bathhouse was a sandy beach and playground. Uncle Dick was put in charge of collecting entry fees to use the bathhouse and the beach. This bathing beach became immensely popular, and people from all over drove in to enjoy the facility.

Second, Jim bought a suspension footbridge that he installed above the dam. This swinging bridge enabled people to access Dick's Side Hill. He also constructed a footpath that zigzagged up the steep slope. Wide spots at intervals along the path were furnished with picnic tables and grills.

The bathhouse faced with rocks from The Creek was adjacent to the swimming beach north of the dam.

Both kids and grownups loved the swimming area that Jim had created.

Now people could visit The Burg, buy provisions at Jim's Inn, swim at the bathhouse and beach, and have a picnic on Dick's Side Hill.

In the winter, there was no swimming because thick ice would form in the lake-like portion of The Creek. This ice was harvested and placed in a newly constructed ice house, run by Dick, to be use in making Jim's Famous Homemade Ice Cream.

This tourism wonderland was quite popular and successful. However, in 1936 a flood nearly wiped everything out, yet Jim rebuilt it all. The playground's death knell came as World War II began and gasoline rationing was implemented. Suddenly, trips from out-of-town just to swim and picnic came to an abrupt stop. The entire enterprise fell into disuse. Years after the War when I was a boy, this tourist spot was open to anyone and was free.

The word "trespassing" didn't mean much to us kids. It wasn't fun to swim in the silted-up near-lake, but the overflow of the dam gouged out a deep swimming hole just below the dam. That became our swimming place of choice.

One evening, several of us rode our bikes to the dam to swim. We were playing tag in the water. Despite it getting dark, the game went on. I heard someone approaching me who might be "it," so I dove in. I hit the rocky bottom and banged my forehead.

Ouch!

No matter. The game went on. An hour later as we biked home, we passed under a street light. Another boy exclaimed about the blood pouring down my face. I went home, washed off the blood, pressed a towel on the wound, lay down on my bed, and fell asleep. Later when my mother arrived home after working the night shift at the hospital, she found me lying in a pool of blood. It must have shocked her.

I did survive and still have a scar in the middle of my forehead. Maybe even like Harry Potter.

Dick's Side Hill became the preferred playground. There was easy access across the footbridge where we could play War, Cowboys and Indians and even Tag.

In the winter we would even attempt sledding on the sloping footpaths. Was it dangerous? Of course. If a sled skidded off the footpath, it meant a steep, fast descent into The Creek. Fortunately, I don't remember anyone ever doing that.

A horse-drawn sleigh would fill up quickly with kids wanting a ride.

So why just one side? If you climbed to the crest of Dick's Side Hill, you could see the other side. But you'd be disappointed. While Dick's Side Hill was steep, heavily forested with footpaths and picnic tables, the other side sloped almost imperceptibly and was covered with a cornfield. It definitely was not as interesting as Dick's Side Hill.

Television came to town when I was a teenager. The Burg was at the bottom of a steep valley, and the nearest TV transmitters were 100 miles away. To get TV broadcasts, you had to put an antenna on the top of Dick's Side Hill and run a cable down the hill, through the forest, across the footbridge and into the house to your television.

Jim's Inn began to sell Philco TVs. Jim' son-in-law, Kenny, installed antennas for everyone who bought a TV. I was Kenny's unpaid helper.

In the beginning, we could get two channels. Channel 6 had the good shows, but was incredibly snowy and hard to watch. Channel 10 had the less good shows, but came in much clearer. Jim's house was the first to be hooked up. My Uncle Cy's house was the second. One by one, other people in town hooked up their houses.

I saved up my money to buy a 17-inch black and white, Philco table model TV for $300 which was a lot of money in those days. I surprised my mother when she came home from work. We had TV! It was wonderful. And it was just another productive use of Dick's Side Hill.

Chapter 11

Revenoors

This story occurred several years after the others in the book, but it paints a picture of the mindset of many of the denizens of the valley in general and The Burg in particular.

After high school, I went off to college where I went on to graduate with an ROTC second lieutenant commission. I was out there in the world serving in our military. During my service, my assignments varied greatly and in each one, I often needed a specific level of security clearance.

Each time I got one of these security clearance needed assignments, I was required to fill out a detailed, three-page form outlining everything I had done up until that point. The last part of form required the names of five people who knew me well enough to provide pertinent information.

Eventually, I got into a situation where I changed military jobs three years in succession. That required three new security clearances. After filling out the extensive paperwork twice, I was tired of filling out the same information. Moreover, I was running out of people to put down as references. So in the third year, I put down the name of The Burg's town drunk.

Wick wasn't really the town drunk since The Burg was a dry town. However, he filled the role of town drunk just the way you would expect a town drunk to be. Wick reminds me of Otis from the *Andy Griffith Show*. Otis was the town drunk, but he was a lovable old sot. Wick did odd jobs round The Burg . He was really a nice guy who was friendly with everyone.

So, I put his name down as a personal reference and turned in the paperwork. Then I got busy and forgot all about it. A few months later, my supervisor told me that the investigation was complete, and I had my new security clearance.

About a year later, I had the opportunity to take military leave and go back to The Burg to visit my mother. The second day I was home, I walked down to Jim's Inn to see who was sitting around drinking coffee.

As I passed a building, I heard, "Pssst." I looked around to see who was trying to get my attention.

It was Wick.

"Hey," he said. "Come over here."

I walked over and greeted him. Wick looked furtively up and down the street. He lowered his voice and said, "A while back, the Revenoors came into town asking a lot of questions about you. Don't worry. I didn't tell them anything."

I thanked him for not telling the Revenoors about me and went on to Jim's Inn.

It was 1944 and I wore a soldier suit to honor of the heroes of the time.

Who knew that I would choose a military career?

Later as I thought about this odd conversation, I realized how well this reflected the people living in the valley and The Burg.

During Prohibition, which was before my time, the area was a hot bed for moonshining. White lightning was produced in enormous quantities throughout the hills and exported to the big cities south and east of The Burg. It was a huge money maker during the Depression for people living in the area, the moonshiners, the bootleggers, and the suppliers of raw materials.

Combating bootleggers and their business was a big government undertaking. Federal law enforcement authorities, collectively called revenoors (or revenuers) by the locals, combed the hills and patrolled the roads looking for bootleg booze and its places of manufacture. The local people saw moonshine as an economic plus and sided with the bootleggers. Their common "enemy" was the revenoors.

Wick was an amiable person who never strayed far from the valley. When the revenoors came to The Burg to question him about me, I'm sure he had no clue why they were doing so. The concepts of security clearance and a background checks were probably alien to him.

To Wick, even a full generation later, these federal officials entering the valley and The Burg were stilled called revenoors and were still treated with suspicion.

Chapter 12

The Front Porch

The houses along Main Street and Water Street had large porches that extended across the entire front of the house. In most instances, the front porch occupied a majority of the space between the house and the sidewalk.

From mid-spring to late-autumn, these front porches served a valuable function. Families, for the most part, lived much of their lives on their

The house in which I grew up photographed recently. If you look closely, you can see the openings between the concrete blocks that make up the porch.

front porches during these pleasant, pre-television days. When it became very warm in mid-summer, the front porch was the refuge where the shade and a light breeze offered some relief from the heat.

Mothers strived to get their kids out of the house, if only to maintain some order and cleanliness inside. So they would shoo the kids outside and onto the porch. Rain or shine, the porch became another playground of sorts.

The front porch was not only for the kids. Our neighbors used their front porch in a way that was typical for the entire town. The neighbors had five children, Beverly, who was a year older than me, and four boys, Dennis, Duane, Douglas and Darryl, all younger than me. Margie, their mother, my mother, and several other women would play Canasta all summer sitting on Margie's front porch. Canasta is a double-deck, rummy-style game that was popular at the time. They would interrupt the day-long canasta game briefly to eat lunch, also on the front porch.

The kids would play on the front porch, sometimes alone, many times with other kids. Duane liked to sit by himself on the banister and watch the daily actions of the people in the town. Most people in the town were rigorously predictable in their daily activities.

For example, John walked down to Jim's Inn every morning at the same time for a cup of coffee and conversation with the town folk. As John passed the porch where Duane was perched.

"Hello, Widget," he would greet Duane.

"My name is Duane," Duane would reply.

Duane was only four years old. This ritual went on each day for months without variation.

Then one day late in the summer, John walked by and said "Hello, Duane."

Stunned, Duane said, "You always call me Widget."

Our front porch was constructed out of decorative concrete blocks that were arranged to have gaps between the blocks, row by row. These gaps provided good sally ports for kids defending the porch during a game of War. Defenders would shoot our toy guns through the gaps in the porch at the attackers outside. The gaps also made wonderful spy holes for the kids as well as for my dog, Tippy, who would keep constant vigil and bark at everyone walking by.

Boys my age tended to congregate on our porch to play games. This was probably because I had quite a few board games, such as Monopoly and Chutes and Ladders. However, we were inventive kids and often made up our own games.

I loved baseball. Fueling this love, my maternal Uncle Bill would supply me with old issues of *The Sporting News*, the bible of baseball. I was eight when I invented a game of baseball that was played using dice. I knew nothing of probability or statistics, but I created this game so we could play baseball on the front porch.

I took the common baseball plays and assigned each to a different roll of the dice. And just like in a real baseball game, there are a more ways to make an out than to get on base.

This is what my house would look like during a typical winter. Here are a few of the neighbor kids posing in the snow.

Years later after taking a probability and statistics class in college, I returned to this childhood game and double checked the probability of the rolls. I discovered that the only roll of the dice that was wildly out of whack compared to the actual probability of happening in a real game was the triple. A dice roll of 12 has a probability of one chance in 36, which is higher than the probability of a triple in a major league game.

The front porch is where people gathered to watch the world go by. There was no television to watch. The houses were not air conditioned. Front porch sitters kept track of every activity in town. Nobody could get away with anything.

I guess this is one of the ways that a small town develops that small town feeling.

Dice Baseball
before learning statistics

Two kids played by each choosing a team. We wrote down the teams' batting lineups. I always went with my favorite team, the Tigers.

Then we alternated throwing the dice - visiting team first and home team second. We would write down what each batter did, just like some people do when they keep score at a live baseball game. At the end of an inning, we would write down the score. A game would normally last about a 30 minutes.

    2: Home run
    3: Double
    4: Single
    5: Rolled as a 4 and 1, error
    5: Rolled as a 3 and 2, ground out
    6: Fly out
    7: Ground out
    8: Ground out
    9: Strike out
    10: Rolled as a 6 and 4, fly out
    10: Rolled as a 5 and 5, double play if there is a
        runner on base
    11: Walk
    12: Triple

Chapter 13

Outdoor Sports

Baseball, or a modified form of it, was the sport of choice at school during the non-snowy days of the school year. Softball, a different form of baseball that uses a larger ball and an underhand pitching technique, dominated the town across the summer.

There was a town softball team. It was made up of young men from The Burg and nearby towns who were six to twelve years older than us kids. The team played their home games at a field in the small village just north of The Burg. They played a game each Sunday, as well as some evenings during the week. No field in the area had lights, so evening games had to start early enough to get done by dusk.

Sunday games, however, were an afternoon affair. Huge numbers of towns folk would pack a picnic lunch, drive the few miles to the field and claim some turf alongside the foul lines to watch the game. The field was mowed just before the game, so the overwhelming smell of freshly cut grass dominated the area.

It was fast-pitch softball and The Burg had a dynamite pitcher named Lee. Lee baffled the opposing team's batters with his delivery. The team was pretty good – or as good as Lee was each game. After the game, if The Burg won, everyone would hop in their cars and drive back to The Burg in a makeshift parade with horns blaring.

We kids used our primary means of transportation – bikes – to go to the game. And after a win, we joined in the raucous parade going back through town.

Many people from town followed the team to their away games, and sometimes we kids would catch rides with the adults to go too. Most of the time our parents didn't know we left town.

One Sunday the town team went to a neighboring town to play, but found two problems when they arrived. First, their scheduled opponent didn't show, so the town team won by a forfeit. Second, another team did show up, claiming they were scheduled to play on that field at that time and their opponent didn't show either.

The problem was resolved when it was suggested that since both teams were there, they should play a game against each other.

Great idea. However, that created another problem. The Burg's team played fast pitch softball, and the other team played slow pitch. The main difference is how the pitcher releases the ball. Fast pitch is a swift, straight underhand pitch that arrives at the batter super fast. Slow pitch is lobbed in an arc that technically must rise higher than the batter's head en route to the plate. From the batter's perspective, the fast pitch seems to be rising while slow pitch is descending.

The last minute game was decided that is would be slow pitch. That neutralized The Burg's team most formidable weapon – Lee's fast pitch wizardry. Lee tried to arc the ball over the plate but was pretty terrible. The Burg's batters tried to hit the descending slow pitch but could not get the timing down enough to make much of an impact.

The Burg's team got smoked.

The kids my age also formed a team and played fast pitch softball. The only opponents we had were the kids at the Kiwanis Camp a couple of miles south of town. The Kiwanis kids couldn't come into town, so all the games were played at the camp. Two evenings a week, we would ride our bikes en masse down the highway to the camp to play a game.

The field at the camp was pretty nice, better than anything we had in town. It had a backstop, real bases and benches for each team to use like a dugout. The only problem was that there was a mature apple tree that grew in the middle of right field. That apple tree required some intricate ground rules.

If the ball hit the trunk, what do we do? Play on! Chase the ball after it ricochets off the tree. If a fly ball got stuck in the branches, then what? Ground rule double and everybody has to go and shake the tree until the ball comes down. Many times I played right field. That statement alone should tell you that I was definitely not the star of our team.

Thinking back to our bike riding to the camp, it amazes me that none of us were ever wiped out riding our bikes on the highway,

And without helmets.

Although I played all the sports with the kids, I certainly was not an athlete. I grew tall but was as skinny as a rail. I am reminded of Charles Atlas and his 97-pound weakling. I wore glasses and was called four eyes. Other boys my age began to bulk up during this time, but not me. I was six feet tall and weighed 120 pounds when I graduated from high school.

Despite this lack of athleticism, I went into my teens and began to notice girls. But that's another story for another chapter.

In the fall, we played football. Football was a choose-up-sides, tackle game that we played in someone's backyard. Both boys and girls played. At this age, the girls were maturing faster than the boys and in some cases were already bigger than we were. It made good sense to have girls on your team, since they could block and tackle better than some boys, including me.

In the winter, we had snowball fights, played pond hockey and rode sleds. For snowball fights, we would chose sides, built forts out of snow, and then clobbered each other with snowballs until we were tired.

We used Gink's pond for pond hockey. The pond was a shallow, wide spot on the millrace, so it froze solid early in the winter and stayed that way until the spring thaw. We had no proper equipment. We created a puck by crushing a tomato soup can flat. We made homemade hockey sticks out of broomsticks and ax handles. We made goals by placing two rocks six feet apart at each end of the pond. Nobody had ice skates. Instead most of us would wear four-buckle arctic boots. There was no protective gear. If you hit the tin can puck with your broomstick just right and it careened off someone's shin, the puck would slice through their jeans and a few layers of skin. I don't think anyone ever got seriously hurt playing pond hockey. However, I'm sure many parents complained about the torn up jeans.

Sledding was probably more dangerous. The best place to sled was Church Street. Church Street started at the top of the hill next to Rocky's Garage on the Bypass and sloped downhill to intersect with Main Street. Jim's Inn was on this corner and it proved to be the busiest part of town.

The protocol was to allow any car or truck to progress down or up Church Street, and then when the coast was clear, belly flop on our sleds headfirst down the street. When the snow cover was just right, your sled could travel the entire length of Church Street and shoot right across Main Street to Jim's Inn. Of course there was traffic on Main Street, but that didn't seem to matter.

Again looking back, I am amazed that nobody got killed.

The more nervous of our siblings would sled elsewhere where it was safer. But I bet they didn't have as much fun as we did on Church Street.

Some kids adhered to the area's more prevalent outdoor sports – hunting and fishing. I never hunted and was an absolute klutz at fishing. A few kids were totally obsessed with these outdoor sports and truly followed the four seasons I described in the opening chapter. Getting ready for hunting season. Hunting season. Getting ready for fishing season. And fishing season. It was fashionable for these kids to wear their hunting and fishing licenses pinned to the back of their jackets at all times.

The boy next door, Duane, was an absolute magician when it came to fishing. He could go to The Creek and with the greatest of ease, pull out several brook trout. He would bring them home for both his mother and my mother. Although cleaning the fish was a chore, the resulting fillets were absolutely scrumptious.

Before I was born, my dad would hunt frequently. In his youth, he and his buddies would do a bit of poaching and hunt deer before hunting season started. One night when they were in the woods stalking deer, they heard a game warden approaching.

"Be very quiet," said my dad. "If that game warden comes over here and starts asking us questions, call me McCracken."

The game warden came over.

You might recall that my dad bet that if George got the roof on his factory before snowfall, he'd change his name to Olmstead. Cousin Buddy held him to that.

Cousin Buddy was on this hunting trip too. And when dad told them guys to call him McCracken, Buddy did that.

For years and years afterwards.

After being banished from the house, we kids played everywhere – on the porch, in the backyard, everywhere in town, up and down the valley, along the highway and on Dick's Side Hill.

Whether we liked it or not, we were truly outdoor kids.

Chapter 14

The Girls

With apologies to Willie Nelson and Julio Iglesias, this chapter is dedicated "to all the girls I've loved before." I was in my preteens and my early teens when I began to notice girls. And I have to say up front, the girls didn't notice me very much.

Back then, I thought everyone living in town belonged to one of the few long-standing tribes that dominated the town, including my own raft of cousins. But now looking back, many of the girls with whom I fell "in love," were from a lot of transient families also.

The first girl I ever noticed in a romantic way was Georgine. She was nine years old to my "mature" ten. She was absolutely beautiful with blue eyes and strawberry-blond, sausage curls. She lived across the street and a few doors down. Even though I was compulsively shy around her, she definitely held my attention. This infatuation ended abruptly when her family moved out of town.

Next door to Georgine's house was the parsonage. One of the many preachers The Burg attracted had two daughters. Jane and Kay were sisters, but Jane won my attention. Not only was she cute, but being a preacher's kid she was very, very good. Her level of goodness might have been off putting to me. Or maybe Jane considered me risky to be around, as I always needed a bath. After a year, Jane and her family moved away. And that was that.

Then it was Judy who caught my eye. Judy's family moved to The Burg to run the hotel. She was a beautiful brunette and had a younger sister named Nancy.

I fell for Judy big time. I would ride my bike to the hotel and hang around just in case she would come around and we could talk.

However, I had competition for Judy's affection. Barry, who came to town each summer from the big city to stay with his grandmother, fell for Judy too. Barry was much bigger than I was. He was growing up and filling out much faster than me. I was still a classic skinny, four-eyed, 97-pound weakling.

One summer our rivalry for Judy's attention got so heated that it came to a head. The showdown happened in the field behind the hotel. Barry and I faced off in a knock-down, drag-em-out fight. Kids from all over town including Judy came to watch.

Barry left the field triumphantly followed by the other kids to celebrate his victory. Judy came over to me as I was lying in the grass with a bloody nose and glasses askew. She was tearful and concerned. She went into the hotel and got a damp cloth to clean up the dirt and blood. Our preteen liaison lasted the rest of the summer.

So I may have lost the fight. But just like in a big Hollywood blockbuster, I won the girl.

After I finished seventh grade with Aunt Mae, the school district decided that The Burg's kids would be bused to the neighboring town for eighth grade and then to high school. That change opened a much wider vista in the pool of kids to get to know.

I vaguely remember the few neighboring town girls in eighth grade that I liked, but for the life of me, I can't remember their names. Those neighboring town kids were soooo much more sophisticated than I was. Even if a budding romance started, the built-in backwardness of me and the sheer logistics of my getting to their town precluded any development of a love life.

However there was finally one girl at the high school who lived in The Burg which improved our possibility for romance. Her name was Karen. She lived at the far north end up on the hill. She was a slim, dark-eyed brunette, and to me she was beautiful. However, she wanted nothing to do with me. She had her eyes set on the star of the basketball team. Ah well. C'est la vie.

I fell for other girls at high school, but since they did not live in The Burg, they are more a part of my story than the story of The Burg.

Aside: I never met another girl named Georgine. However many years later, I met a young woman named Judy who shared a house with a nurse named Jane. Judy and I got married and had one daughter. My only daughter's name is Karen.

My cousins, The 4C's. Left to right, Carolyn, Claramae, Connie and Cynthia in front.

There were other girls in The Burg, of course, but most of them were my cousins. Four of my cousins lived next door and since we grew up together, they were more like sisters than cousins. Each girl was beautiful in her own way. There were two brunettes and two blondes. All smart as whips. They were Uncle Cy's daughters known as the 4C's – Carolyn, Connie, Claramae and Cynthia. I was the same age as Claramae.

Together we would play "girl stuff" like house and paper dolls. My mother tried to get me to take tap dance with Claramae, but I was the quintessential klutz and not very motivated. Claramae and Cynthia became highly accomplished in tap. The girls also had some musical talent and played in the high school band. I tried out for the band on clarinet. And the band director said I could march in the band, but I was not to make any noise with that horn. I decided that band was not worth it.

During high school, all the neighbors would sit on their respective porches and eyeball all the boys who came to pick up Connie or Claramae for a date. The neighbors would of course register their approval or disapproval of the swain.

One summer Connie came home from college. At the time she was dating Budd with two Ds. But the son of the current preacher ask Connie out anyways. His name was Bud with one D. When Bud with one D came to pick up Connie, the youngest of the 4C's, Cynthia, looked up, confused.

She asked in a loud, stage whisper, "Why are there two Bud(d)s?"

Beverly also lived next door, but on the other side from the 4C's. She was a year older than me and the eldest of her family. She had four brothers and seeing that she was the eldest, her mother often put her in charge of the boys. She was a built-in babysitter, so to speak.

The boys were rambunctious as one might expect and ran amok in the town-wide playground. While Beverly did a pretty good job controlling her brothers, she did have a secret weapon – her father Don. One summer afternoon, Don was sunning in his backyard. The boys were running around ripping and snorting and Beverly lost control. At her behest, Don simply sat straight up and stared at the boys. Amazingly, as if struck by the Holy Spirit itself, all four boys instantly became perfect angels.

There were other girls in town like Janie, Jeannie Sue, Nancy, the twins Mary and Helen, Florence, Shirleen, Carol, Sally, Della Mae and Donna

Kay. The memories attached to them have faded over time. And there were probably other girls, who have forever left my memory.

Maybe that's a good thing.

At least from their point of view.

Chapter 15

The Boys

As I went from a child to a teenager, my interest shifted from playing with the boys to checking out the girls. So obviously, the previous chapter was much more fun to both live through and write. Yet, for balance, may I introduce the boys.

Adult supervision was practically nonexistent. There seemed to be very few limitations or restrictions on our activities around town. We held no value in signs marked "No Trespassing" or "Private Property." We treated the every square inch of The Burg as our playground. Well, except the insides of the houses as even we were not allowed in our own houses during the day.

2016 Presidential candidate Bernie Sanders talks about in his book *Our Revolution*, the "profound lesson about democracy and self-rule" he learned as a boy on the streets of Brooklyn. "Nobody supervised us. Nobody coached us. Nobody refereed our games. We were on our own. Everything was organized and determined by the kids themselves. The group worked out our disagreements, made all the decisions, and learned to live with them."[4]

4. Sanders, B. (2018). *Our revolution: A future to believe in.* New York: Thomas Dunne Books, St. Martins Press.

This was exactly how it was in The Burg when I was growing up.

Bicycles gave us freedom. Safety was not an issue. We rode in packs on the Bypass highway with little concern about the cars and trucks flying by, horns blaring.

Not all of the boys rode bikes. Millard lived north of The Burg by a few miles and did not have a bike, so he improvised. Millard came to town by way of the highway driving a riding lawn mower. He would drive the lawn mower down to Jim's Inn to see his buddies and to eat ice cream.

Millard sometimes stayed at Jim's Inn late and had to ride home in the dark. Some people pointed out that this was very unsafe especially on the highway. Millard could get run over by an unsuspecting car or truck. Ever the adaptable, Millard rectified this the next day. He showed up at Jim's Inn just like he had every other day, but this time he had with him two flashlights. When it was time to go home for the night, he saddled up on his riding mower, put one flashlight in each hip pocket of his bib overalls and turned them on. Millard never had a problem driving his mower on the highway after that.

There were a lot of boys in The Burg. One group was older than me – Ben, Gail, Clair, Buddy, John, Kline, Harry, Kim, David and Norman. One group was my age – Max, Chick, Ellery, the two Tommys, Frank, John and Jon. And I hung out with boys in both groups.

I was thrilled when Buddy would ask me to help make ice cream for Jim's Inn. My favorite flavor to make was cherry vanilla. I got to stir the maraschino cherries into the vanilla ice cream. Yum!

Ben was another one of my many cousins and son of our school teacher. He taught me how to drive in a World War II Jeep. Our lessons would take place in the fields at the game preserve just north of town.

Frank and one of the Tommys were brothers. When their mother was in the hospital having her fourth child, the family gathered. The youngest bother was asked the newborn's name.

He replied, "His name is George, but we call him Georgie for short."

Another family in The Burg had three boys all around my age. The eldest was named Donald followed by David and Dean. Donald was my age. All three boys would join in the activities of The Burg, but what they really found important was hunting.

The brothers took hunting season (and getting ready for hunting season) very seriously. It was the pinnacle of each year. They would pack up camping gear, purchase ammunition, clean their guns, set up the deer blind and apply for the hunting license.

The hunting license was a three inch by four inch piece of paper issued by the state. Hunters bought a license holder made out of leather and isinglass, so they could display their license while hunting, as was required. They would pin the leather license holder to the back of their hunting jacket right between the shoulder blades.

Donald and his two brothers went beyond that. To them, possessing a hunting license was a badge of honor. They attached their licenses to the back of any shirt or jacket they wore. They wore their licenses for all occasions.

And they weren't the only ones. For those people who revered hunting above all, wearing the license year round was their way of offering testimony to this wonderful season.

The first day of deer season was a school holiday. If it wasn't, many students and teachers alike would have been absent. Thousands of deer hunters both local and from the big cities, would be decked out in their expensive, camouflaged hunting outfits. The camouflage was to keep the deer from seeing the hunters. But it always seemed incongruous, however, that each hunter also wore bright orange on their hunting caps.

If deer can see colors or sheer brightness, the orange hat would surely give the hunter away. Obviously, the orange caps was to alert other hunters that the wearer of the hat was human, not a deer. In these woods, getting shot by another hunter was a bigger risk than getting attacked by a deer.

Each year Cousin Bobby would win the unofficial prize for the most hickory-stick paddlings at school. Outside of school, he was a hellion.

On Halloween, Bobby would join the older boys trick-or-treating around town. Then candy was not the prime objective – damage and destruction were, and Bobby fit right in. Halloween lasted three weeks in The Burg. Each night, boys marauded through town, trick-or-treating. Many times they would just dispense tricks. The most common trick they played was soaping both house and car windows. They would take a bar of Ivory Soap and smear it on the windows and the screens.

In October, the maple trees that lined Main Street, would drop their leaves. The boys would see this as another opportunity to play tricks. They would gather fallen leaves and deposit them on front porches. Certain houses got extra leaves. The amount of leaves was a direct ratio to the amount of complaints about trick-or-treating from that house.

One Halloween, the older boys decided to knock over outhouses. As this was in concert with Bobby's wild personality, he went along to help.

A typical outhouse was pretty sturdy. They were small wooden structures that straddled a pit with one or two places to sit inside. Most outhouses were firmly anchored, usually to a foundation surrounding the pit.

Knocking over an outhouse was hard work. It took several of the older, bigger boys and a lot of effort to push over an outhouse. But Bobby helped. The older boys who experienced at the craft, would stop pushing when the outhouse began to topple. New to the game, Bobby did not stop pushing. He kept it pushing as hard as he could and continued to walk forward.

He ended up in the pit, up to his waist in…well…

Chapter 16

Go Home Again?

No.

Thomas Wolfe says in his novel of the same name, "You Can't Go Home Again." His book is about a writer who writes a book but makes copious references about his hometown. The residents of the town didn't like the way the author depicted them, which they viewed as a distorted version of them and the town. The sent him hate letters and death threats.

I went back to The Burg several times when my mother lived there. After she passed, I go less often. When I do go, I stay with my cousin Connie. She catches me up on the town gossip. She tells me the things and places that have changed and what the remaining relatives are up to. We travel around The Burg, visit old friends and other cousins, swap old stories and enjoy each other's company.

Not many relatives are left. Seeing them is becoming even more important to me over time. We visit Claramae and Carolyn, Connie's sisters. They are the surviving members of the 4C's. Carolyn lives in the house where she and her sisters grew up which is next door to the house where I grew up.

My house has changed hands a few times since my mother moved out. From the street, it looks much the same as it did when I was a kid. And it is apparent at first glance that front porch living is still in vogue.

One of my favorite people to visit is cousin Nonie, who is a bit older than me. Nonie lives with her son. She is spry and fun to talk to. She says that she likes takes a nip or two of the hard stuff a few times during the day. She says it keeps her going.

I also like to see Cousin Buddy. He is Nonie's age and is still active and bubbly.

Several years ago, my colleague and I went to a conference in one of the big cities south of The Burg. After the conference, we rented a car and drove up to The Burg and stayed at Connie's house. My colleague grew up

Connie, me and Claramae, taken much later on one of my return visits to The Burg.

in another state and was unfamiliar with small town living in a place like The Burg.

Connie and I set up a get together at a restaurant in a nearby town. Many people from The Burg including Nonie and Buddy came. The waitress at the restaurant was high school aged. She took our orders. Buddy ordered a steak. She asked him how would he like it prepared. Buddy blushed and stammered. He couldn't say exactly what he wanted.

Nonie jumped in and exclaimed, "He wants the center to be titty pink."

I could not keep my mouth shut, so I said to the waitress, "Make sure you show the cook exactly how he wants his steak."

She turned bright red and got a funny look on her face. She replied, "He's my father."

My colleague laughed so hard he fell out of his chair.

My recent visits to The Burg have usually happened in winter. I walk the length of a freshly plowed Main Street, and take in all that has changed and all that has stayed the same. Several houses have fallen into disrepair. Many have been bought, I assume by people from the nearby city, and have undergone substantial renovation.

Jim's Inn is gone. Jim's grandchildren and great-grandchildren sold everything including Dick's Side Hill to a company from a neighboring town. They have gentrified Jim's Inn. They still make and sell ice cream, thus preserving a long tradition.

There is a new combination gas station and convenience store near the intersection of Church Street and the Bypass. I suppose that local folks might have moved to that Quickie Mart for their morning meeting of coffee drinking and discussion of important things.

The swinging bridge and the dam are gone. The Creek flows unfettered again as it did in the early 1930's. Dick's Side Hill still looms over the town's eastern horizon, but it is hard to get there now.

The sawmill is still there with The Creek flowing by. Early on, the people running the sawmill would create a sawdust pile along the banks of The Creek. The sawdust deteriorated into its chemical components, seeped into The Creek and killed the trout. No more. Compliments of state regulations, the sawmill is required to dispose of its sawdust in an environmentally favored way. The Creek is again clean and filled with trout.

The meat packing plant, owned and sold off by my father and his brothers, burned down. It was replaced by a smaller facility. The retail meat store is gone.

There is a motorcycle repair shop just north of the house with the Ivaroy.

The Methodist church is still going strong.

The old school and the Brand X Factory were repurposed into small apartments.

The maple trees that lined Main Street were sacrificed to widen the street.

The individuals living in The Burg have changed. Old folks have passed away. New families have moved in. New kids are growing up there like I did. Sorta. These kids go to a modern, regional school south of The Burg instead of a one room, one teacher school. Most likely they are not participating in rote learning and sing-song recitation either. I don't know if the kids have incorporated the whole town as their playground like we did, or not.

The terrain is the same. Even with global warming, the meteorology of The Burg seems the same – hot and humid in the summer, cold and snowy in the winter, with long, wet springs and glorious falls.

The feeling to me is the same. I can go to The Burg to visit, but I don't think I could go home permanently. The protagonist in Thomas Wolfe's book summed it up:

> "You can't go back home to your family, back home to your childhood ... back home to a young man's dreams of glory and of fame ... back home to places in the country, back home to the old forms and systems of things which once seemed everlasting but which are changing all the time – back home to the escapes of time and memory."

There is a country song titled "You Are Always 17 In Your Home Town." You go away and mature. For the folks back home, their image of you is based on the last time they saw you. The reverse is true, too. The Burg is a place that stands unchanged in my mind. It remains as it was when I ventured out of the valley as a youth.

The Burg was an ideal place to grow up. I surprised myself at how many memories I conjured out of my subconscious. When I returned to The Burg over the years, I visited with my cousins and they inspired more wonderful memories.

As this book ends, unlike Thomas Wolfe's protagonist, I anticipate no hateful letters or death threats.

Chapter 17

Gallimaufry

This chapter is a collection of pictures that I feel need to be included. There is no running narrative, thus it is a gallimaufry, or "hodge-podge." Included are pictures of grandparents, of my mother and father, of uncles, of cousins, and of neighbor kids. There are several of me. Let them help document an era that has long passed. An era that was very good to me.

Brothers Mike, Cy and Jake.

Me and my parents, Lavina and Mike.

My maternal grandparents Huldah and Joseph and me. They lived in another town 36 miles north of The Burg.

My mother, Lavina.

My father, Mike.

Lavina and Mike.

My high school graduation, 1955.

102

Back row, left to right: Ruth, Mae, Cy, Martha, Mom-poo, Pop-poo and a hired hand.
Front row, left to right: Clarice, Roy, Jake, Lester and Mike.

Me and my cousins, Connie, Claramae and Carolyn.

103

My father in the cooler at the meat packing plant.

104

Meat packing plant's entire fleet of trucks with Jake's house behind them.

Cy showing off a new truck for the fleet.

George, Mike, Cy and Jake in the plant with the heavy equipment.

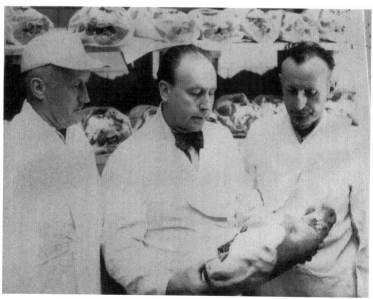

Jake, Cy, and Mike admiring a ham.

106

Me bundled up for winter.

My mother had just bought me a new snow suit.

This is often what Main Street would look like after the snow plow came through.

Denny who lived next door at the bathing beach.

Me and my second cousin, Jolie, Roy's granddaughter.

Cousin Connie with her doll.

Cousin Connie in a new snowsuit.

Me ready to play baseball in our back yard. Clearly been a fan all my life.

Me walking Main Street next to the maple trees as the snow melted.

Me with my maternal grandmother's dog, Pat.

My house and my mother after a big snowfall.

110

Acknowledgments

All of the tales in this book are true or are as true as tales augmented by years and years of enjoyable retellings can be. Some of these stories became legends recounted through the years by my mother and my uncles Jake and Cy. If any inaccuracies have crept in, they are the fault of time and the nature of oral history.

I want to thank my cousins, Claramae, Buddy, Nonie and Carolyn, and especially Connie who was a prime contributor to many of these stories.

The photos come from old collections and old friends. Connie's son, Todd, helped greatly in curating many of these images.

And I want to thank my daughter, Karen, who tirelessly laid out this book and helped me get it published.

Made in the USA
Middletown, DE
25 July 2020

13702089R00073